Wor
Comprenending Love

By
Clarence Kenny Plank II

All of Clarence Kenny Plank II poetry books can be found on Amazon.com and on his personal website www.shoeboxpoet.com
Sign up for his newsletter.

Here is a listing of other titles by the author:
Finding Peace Within the Storm.
The Shoebox Poet.
Writer of Wrongs.
Poems From A Heart Shaped Box.

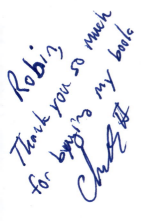

You can follow him on:
Youtube: ShoeboxPoet
Twitter: @ShoeboxPoet
Facebook: @Shoeboxpoet45
Instagram: @nitejokertn

List of Content:

Lost
It was your eyes,
When I first saw you,
That made me realize,
I wanted to spend,
My life,
Gazing into them,
And being lost,
In your soul.

Time
It is time to celebrate,
To all the good times,
We have been through,
The years,
As we grow older together,
And deeper in love.

Making
It was your laugh,
That made me,
Like you,
But,
It was your heart,
That made me,

Fall in love with you.

Growing Old
After years,
Of being,
Great friends,
Telling secrets,
And sharing,
Laughs,
It is nice to know,
I can grow old,
With a friend like you.
I love you,
With all that,
I am.
Every piece,
Of my heart.
Going through life,
It is best,
To have a close friend,
You can,
Spend time with.

Spots
Fishing buddies,
And beer,
Those stories,
Had to start someplace.

Tripping

Did it hurt,
When you fell,
Into my waiting arms,
Don't feel bad,
I tripped,
Over that step,
Yesterday too.

Hers
Is a temple,
A place,
Of worship,
A holy place,
Where life,
Begins,
And radiates,
It's hope,
Renewed,
Only angels,
Reside there,
Lorded over,
By a goddess,
Because,
Her body,
Is sacred,
An untouched,
Alter,
For which,
She has command,
So who,
Are you?
To think,
Or believe,
She belongs,

To you,
That her soul,
Her heart,
And mind,
Were laid,
Claim by you?
This goddess,
Can do whatever,
She wants,
With her temple,
If she wants kids,
Then she will,
Let life begin,
If not,
There are other,
Means for her to love,
Her mind is hers,
Because,
You, in your infancy,
Can't change her mind,
Her soul is hers,
And I pity the man,
Who touches it,
Unless,
You want to lose,
Your mind,
Her heart is hers,
Don't risk,
Taking it,
If you are not,
Going to place yours,
On her alter,
As a sacrifice,
Because,
You can't change her,
Body and mind,

They are hers alone,
If she wants long hair,
Or short,
Maybe bald or what,
It's her choice,
If a goddess,
Wants the world,
To know how,
Dangerous her curves,
Can truly be,
Then you better,
Hold on tight,
When your making love,
To the temple,
Of a goddess.

Universe
You have stars,
Coursing through,
Your veins,
The cosmos,
Spiraling in your eyes,
As I taste,
All the galaxies,
You have blessed,
With the sound,
Of your voice,
When I kiss you,
Running my fingers,
Through your hair,
Knowing those strands,
Hold planets,
In place,
As we embrace,

I feel the warmth,
Of your heart,
Beating like the sun,
At the center,
Of your universe,
As I explore,
The farthest reaches,
Of your inner space,
Making love to the cosmos,
Of your divine beauty.

Gaze
My fingers,
Laced together,
In yours,
I spent,
Years,
Chasing after you,
And here,
We are,
As I gaze,
Into your eyes,
And the flames,
Of your heart,
Rise,
Holding you,
While I'm drowning,
Under you,
As I kiss you,
The ache,
Hurts,
Like someone,
Is turning a knife,
Digging into me.

Drowning

I'm dancing all around,
Without you,
Missing pieces,
Falling around me,
As I come apart,
The waters coming in,
But you're nowhere to be found,
So, here I am,
Drowning in your sea,
Without you,
As I sink beneath the waves,
Breathing in the mist,
Swirling around,
Tasting the salt,
Of my tears,
Holding onto your ghost,
Drifting with the tide,
Wishing you,
Were here,
To rescue me,
As I drown in you,
Watching you fade.

You

Came into my life,
And made it,
Meaningful again,
As I held your hand,
I couldn't imagine,
Where you didn't exist,

In my world,
After that night,
I wanted to hold you,
Tightly in my arms,
Because letting go,
Meant,
Goodbye,
However short it was,
Spending an hour,
Was not enough,
Looking into your eyes,
Under your mask,
Deep blue,
Like mine,
And a soul,
Belonging to someone,
I felt like I knew,
For a lifetime,
Just by holding,
You in my arms.

Paid
What am I worth?
It's a question,
I often ask myself,
For you,
To spend time with me,
How do you value,
Your time with someone?,
Is it dollars or cents?,
Seeing someone as a client,
Instead of a friend,
When business relationships,
Turn into something more,

Or wish it was,
Something more,
Than a passing fling.

◆ ◆ ◆

The Dancing Woman
She's a woman,
In a pretty dress,
Her name is Karma,
We've been dancing,
For a little while,
As she holds me,
Tightly in her arms,
She whispers,
In my ear,
Of my deeds,
They weren't wrongs,
It's the price,
You have to pay,
For loving too much,
In the way,
That you are,
She told me,
Love is a like fountain,
Of cool water,
You will not drink from,
Unless you,
Find a woman,
Who will love your flaws,
And how broken,
You are,
I whispered back,
Then I will love you,
Since you're the only woman,
Here in my

Stars
I want you,
To feel you,
As I trace,
The stars,
Beneath your skin,
And connect,
The dots,
Of the constellations,
Along your curves,
Searching the heavens,
In your secret places,
As we lay awake,
Gliding my fingers,
Over your skin,
As I touch,
The universe,
Within you.

Armor
It's tough,
Moving on,
When a piece,
Of you wants,
To remain,
And stand,
Watch,
Over a person,
Who found,
A way,
Into your life,

By piercing,
Your armor,
Surrounding,
Your heart,
I guess,
Some walls,
Are meant,
To be broken,
Down or worn,
Away,
Avoiding you,
Doesn't make,
The pain go away,
Seeing your face,
Only makes,
The ache,
Worse,
When my heart,
Chooses,
You from the start,
Where my heart,
Remembers,
Your touch,
And knowing,
You're out there,
In the world,
And here I am,
Not even ready,
To lace up,
My own shoes,
To be with you,
Because I missed,
My chance,
To find forever,
With you.

◆ ◆ ◆

Pride
There are times,
When I hear your voice,
Inside my head,
When I find myself down,
You may not be here,
Where I can hug you,
But I know you're watching,
Over us every day,
With a big smile,
And just gleaming,
With the pride of a mother,
As your kids,
Work hard to pursue,
Their dreams,
And doing their best,
To take care of each other,
Because in this life,
You did your best,
To raise us,
I miss you every day,
But I remember,
The good times we shared,
And how much,
You loved to laugh,
I love you mom.

Harden
For all the bad times,
And heartaches,
Life throws at us,

Breaking us down,
We are giving choices,
In how we choose,
To reflect ourselves,
Through the pain,
Of life, Older souls,
Understand this,
Because their journey,
Through life,
Has made them immortal,
But not harden,
By the sadness of things,
Carry your light,
Shine bright,
Even in darkness,
There is a light,
Glowing like a beacon.

Offerings
When I found you,
I wasn't expecting,
Things to be this way,
It's like magic,
Because I came to you,
As a friend,
And expecting very little,
In return,
Since this is the way,
It is with other people,
When most people,
Offer me a planet,
And I accepted,
You are different,
So much more,

Because in return,
You gave me a galaxy,
Along with your heart,
And for that,
I'm truly grateful,
For you.

Vastness
She has the cosmos,
Coursing through her,
She breathed in light,
And exhaled stars,
Throughout the universe,
When we touched,
It was like a bomb,
Went off,
As I drank from her soul,
And tasted,
Stardust from her lips,
Holding her in my arms,
We created life,
Within our galaxy.

Part 1
The doctor's said,
It was fatal,
What I had,
With only days,
To live,
As I looked,
Out the window,
Four days,

You're on the clock son,
Where do I begin,
Making peace,
Reaching out,
To family and friends,
Letting them know,
But being so far away,
And too broke,
To travel home,
I sat in my room,
With three days,
Remaining,
Going through,
Old photographs,
Then I see her smile,
Peering back at me,
The one that got away,
I remembered her,
And how she tasted,
When we kissed,
Suddenly,
I found myself,
Making my way East,
It's been years since,
I last held her,
We had a falling out,
But mended fences,
Late night chats,
And Saturday phone calls,
Until one day,
She stopped calling,
Her page updated,
But she wouldn't respond,

Days turned into weeks,
Months and then a year,
Two days were left,
As my car crossed,
Into the state she lived in.

Part 2
Pulling up to her place,
The memories,
Came flooding back,
As I saw visions of us,
Laying in the grass,
Counting the stars,
Or you holding me,
In the swing on your porch,
Lazy summers,
And chilly nights,
Found us,
Falling deeper,
Into each other's arms,
Ringing the door bell,
My heart leaped,
Into my throat,
When you came,
To answer the door,
Your hair was longer,
Straight blonde,
Cool pools of blue,
Shined brightly,
As you peered,
Out of the screen door,
A smile,

Crossed your lips,
As you met me,
You held me,
In your arms,
And I felt,
Like I was home again,
But your kiss,
Was so much more,
Than I remembered,
Drinking from your lips.

Part 3
She,
Was here,
In my arms again,
And there,
It was magic,
For the first time,
In days,
I wanted to live,
She had gotten busy,
And lost touch,
Met a guy,
And fallen out of love,
While picking up the pieces,
We made dinner together,
As she told me about things,
We shared laughs,
And spent the night,
Talking about life,
I didn't have the heart,
To tell her,

It was selfish of me,
As I thought to myself,
Laying in the bed,
The next morning,
With her,
One day left,
We made love,
Last night,
It just happened,
This time,
Out of all the other times,
I felt passion,
Burn between us,
As I made love to her,
I took my time,
Because I wanted,
It to last for the both of us,
One good solid memory,
We spent the day,
Enjoying each other's company,
I told her,
I was travelling up the coast,
Just enjoying my vacation,
And I was leaving out,
In the morning.

Part 4
While she slept,
I wrote her a letter,
Telling her everything,
And telling her,
How much I regretted,

The decision,
To find her,
When she deserved,
So much more,
Telling her about my illness,
And I only had hours,
To live,
I wanted her to know,
Where she could find me,
As I packed up my things,
Kissed her goodbye,
And drove out to the coast,
I built a small fire,
While sitting on the shore,
I could hear the surf,
As it pounded the sand,
Looking up at the stars,
I saw a shooting star,
And made a wish,
Morning slowly came,
As I sat watching,
The colors change,
Until the sun appeared,
Over the horizon,
I felt numb,
As a tear,
Ran down my cheek,
Things started getting blurry,
As I felt my heart racing,
And everything,
Went black.

Part 5
I awoke,
Laying her arms,
Her eyes,
Were puffy,
As a tear drop,
Fell upon my cheek,
She cupped my face,
In the palm of her hand,
Leaning in to kiss me,
It was deep,
Long,
And heart felt,
I reached my arms,
Around her,
Embracing her,
Drawing her closer,
We stood up together,
Watching the waves,
Roll along the shore,
The wind gathered her hair,
Around her face,
She stared back at me,
With those blue eyes,
I went home with her,
As we talked,
The phone rang,
And the doctor,
Was calling to tell me,
He gave me the wrong report,
That I was going to live,
As anger,
Climbed into my voice,

I stopped,
Looking into her eyes again,
I thanked him,
And hung up,
Dropping down to one knee,
I asked her to marry me.

◆ ◆ ◆

Orange
Madness?
What is this?
A simple song,
Of torture,
And malice,
Those vandals,
So melancholy,
In their wrath,
Those three,
Brazen thugs,
Terrorizing people,
In their homes,
The madness,
Of it all.

◆ ◆ ◆

Old Flame
It's been over twenty years,
Since you and I met,
And you still dog my steps,
Why is that?
I know you're watching me,
All over social media,
Because you hide yourself,

You're the only person,
From my past,
Who sets their stuff to private,
To stalk an old boyfriend,
You do realize,
I'm not that person I was back then,
I've buried those bodies,
Of the people I used to be,
Either by choice,
By murder,
Or suffering,
To put myself,
Out of my misery,
So, now why are you here?,
Did I father your child?
And that is the reason,
You keep close tabs on me?
Or are you so possessive,
Of something that doesn't belong to you?
And regret letting me go?
I'm human, I belong to myself,
That piece of me I gave to you,
Died a long time ago,
I would be lying,
If I said I didn't fully care,
A part of me did wanted you to stay,
I didn't want an open relationship,
Nor did I want a long distance one,
I wanted to continue our friendship,
Somehow, you made it into a game,
Trying to control me,
So, here we dance again,
I don't want you,
The last time we talked,
You were married,
Did you get a divorce?

Why are you coming around?
There's nothing here for you?
You're not going to find closure here,
All it's going to do is piss you off,
When you learn the truth,
That I didn't go looking for you,
Wonder how you're doing?
I don't even check up on my ex-fiancée,
So, what does that tell you?
I've learned to let go of my past,
Forgive myself and move on,
You need to do the same,
Holding onto the past,
Only hurts your future,
Let me go.

Deep
Here is your notice,
You have been evicted,
From my heart and mind,
And never to linger here,
I am not a booby prize,
Or a consolation trophy,
I am so much more,
You would not understand this,
If you gave me a chance,
I would have loved you,
With a love so deep,
Because it is without measure,
It would have eased your scars,
And wiped away your tears,
I would have protected you,
In these arms,

Kept you warm,
And you've would have known,
You were the only one,
For the rest of our lives,
As I choose you,
To spend my life with.

Pages
She is a poem,
Waiting for a man,
To write prose,
On the pages,
In her heart.

Colors
I wonder,
What it would be like,
To kiss a blonde,
If her lips tasted like,
A crisp winter morning,
The ones,
Where you lounge,
By the fire,
Drinking hot chocolate,
While gazing into her eyes,
Maybe a redhead,
To see if it's true,
She is fire made flesh,
So, would my lips burn,
When we kissed,
Like kissing a flame?

Brunette haired beauties,
Are divine,
They smell of lavender,
And roses,
Sprinkled by morning dew,
Laced with delicate kisses,
I've kissed raven haired women before,
But none like you,
Would your lips,
Taste like honey,
Perhaps?
Or maybe they taste like love,
If it could be described as such,
Considering it's a feeling,
That I haven't experienced,
Where a woman,
Returns my love,
Because all the experiences,
I have,
None could compare,
To holding you,
In my arms,
And drinking from your mind,
As we touched lips,
But I guess,
That's why,
There wouldn't be,
Many novels,
Written about,
Murder mysteries,
If it was based off experiences.

So Close
There's something,

About her,
I'm mesmerized,
By the beauty,
Of the woman,
As she sits,
Only a few feet from me,
I'm fighting so hard,
Not to stare,
At this woman,
It's just the way,
Her hair falls,
Around her shoulders,
Those ruby red lips,
As they move,
When she talks,
And I melt,
When I see her smile,
Her laugh,
Is exciting,
Because it fills me with joy,
I guess you could call it that,
All I know,
It's intoxicating,
Being this close to her,
And feeling her warmth,
Like basking in the glow,
Of the sun,
On a summers day,
And that dress,
Black and sleek,
Hugging her curves,
Nothing daring,
But modest,
It's enough,
To make you notice her,
Ah shit,

She noticed me,
Staring at her,
And she smiled,
Did she just wink at me?

Rivers
Her mind,
Is like a river,
And it branches,
Off into streams,
Of thoughts,
Daydreams,
And ideas,
Romance,
And adventure,
Of grand designs,
Mystery,
And passion,
She's intelligent,
A spark,
Beautiful,
Without bounds,
She's everything,
A man should desire,
In a woman,
But only a few men,
Deserve her,
Because her mind,
Is a bountiful,
Playground,
Of wonders,
And excitement,
Just like her heart,
Both need to be loved,

And cared for,
Touched often,
In so many ways,
But not with your fingers,
Or with your hands,
But gently,
With words,
And understanding,
For her mind,
Like her soul,
Is wild,
Untamed,
And for someone like me,
I drank from your waters,
Just in passing,
And it was enough,
To make me realized,
How thirsty I was,
For a woman like you.

Inches
Intimacy,
Isn't about sex,
It's about finding passion,
And the feeling of touch,
Or being touched,
In places where,
By evolution,
We were meant,
To feel the touch,
Of another person,
It's nature,
We've forgotten these things,
As we hold the curves,

Of our phones,
In the palm of our hands,
Touching a glow screen,
When another person,
Who longs for your touch,
Is only inches away from you.

◆ ◆ ◆

Healing
When despair,
Comes rushing in,
And loneliness,
Is your only friend,
Times change,
As you find yourself,
Looking inside,
From the mirror,
Deep within,
No regrets,
Will be left in me,
As I step into,
Something new,
Leaving behind,
That broken man,
Healing my scars,
And stepping free,
From the cocoon,
Two men stand,
The old,
With the new,
Only time,
Will tell,
For me to learn,
To fly,
With my wings somehow,

And new dreams come,
As old ones die.

Being Ourselves
Is there someplace,
Some space,
Where we can go,
To talk about it all,
And how everything,
Is the same,
Being apart,
Being distant,
From ourselves,
As we try to find a way,
To relate,
And navigate,
All these twists and turns,
We call life,
Because we're both striving,
For the same prize,
The same outcome,
In trying to love each other,
Without harming,
Or alarming,
The other,
We were meant,
To be together,
So why is it so hard,
For you to open your eyes,
And see me standing here,
Before you,
Wishing you,
Would hold me,
Show me,

All the love you possess,
Instead of hiding it,
Or wasting it on fools.

Core

Will she,
Want to peel away,
The layers of me?
Down to the core,
Where all the hurt lies,
Not to heal me,
But understand,
How deep my wounds go,
So they will become scars,
Under the touch,
Of her love,
Where I can have,
A safe place to thrive,
And grow into the man,
She needs me to be.

Tame

Women want bad boys,
An art project to tame,
Turning beast into man,
What they fail to realize,
Some men are lost causes,
So, they burn out with them,
But good guys,
Are bland,
And boring as fuck,
Really,

Did you know bad boys,
Were once good guys,
Who were burned,
By some woman,
Tearing away their hearts,
And beating down their souls,
All these guys did,
Was find away,
To break someone else,
With the pain some woman,
Caused them.

Wrinkles
I remember you,
The way your hair,
Lays behind your ear,
When you brushed it back,
The way your eyes,
Light up,
When you smile,
And how the wrinkles,
Of your laugher,
Shows the curves,
In your face,
The feeling of your touch,
As I hold you,
Even for a few seconds,
Is a memory,
I run over,
And over in my head,
How you smelled,
The scent of your perfume,
Or maybe your soap,
Made my senses,

Explode,
Every time I was near you,
Or trailing behind you,
Collecting pieces of you,
Remembering,
The little things you do,
So, I can replay them,
When I recalled you,
Into my mind,
To help me,
Understand who you are,
Without saying a word,
Because I am,
Too shy,
To ask you,
And too afraid,
Of what you would say,
To someone like me,
Who's in love,
With a memory,
Of the time,
We spent together.

Unlike
You touched my mind,
With your words,
Before your fingers,
Touched my skin,
And your arms,
Hugged me,
For the very first time,
You're unlike,
So, many other women,
In how you,

Show yourself,
To people you love,
Because,
You don't play games,
Mess with someone's head,
You're honest,
But this is what you expect,
From the people,
You let into your world,
Your love is true,
And pure,
As you help build me up,
To show me,
How the broken pieces,
Of my past,
And my heart,
Should fit,
Together to form,
Someone new,
To present to the world,
Where I can love,
Myself and others,
Without fear,
And having the courage,
To be strong,
In the face of adversity,
Even if I am alone,
Because if it wasn't for you,
There would be no me,
And I am so thankful,
For you.

Power
We are made of water,

Water is power,
It has enough force,
To crumble walls,
Buildings,
Roads and bridges,
All at once,
Or slowly,
Overtime,
Eroding away,
The foundations,
Slipping through cracks,
But it is the most gentle,
It can wash away pride,
Drown your ego,
Put out fires,
Brings life,
And carries it,
Deep within its depths,
Yet, it is not afraid,
To touch the broken,
Rinse away sins,
And heal the living,
Not many people,
Realize this.

Fancy
You're the definition,
Of elegance,
If it was made flesh,
Someone who,
Enjoys the fancy side,
Of the things,
That life has to offer,
Because you work hard,

So those things,
These pleasures,
Are yours to behold,
And I find myself,
Astounded,
Watching you,
Live your life,
It makes me want that,
A care free life,
Of worry,
But you probably have those too,
Only you hide it from everyone,
You're still human.

Dancing Souls
Dancing in the dark,
The music beats,
Mimicking your heartbeat,
I still feel your kiss,
As it haunts my lips,
It was spell bounding,
When I drew you closer?
Sometimes words,
Are not enough,
As we lace our fingers together,
Touch is a language of its own,
I held you so close,
Our souls seemed to dance,
Being so close to you,
Feeling things,
Like we were writing tales,
Creating galaxies,
As we touched,
Because your fingertips,

Aroused my soul,
From it slumber,
And I find,
I am restless without you,
As my soul,
Refuses to sleep again.

Herself
She hides,
The tears she cried,
As she puts on,
Her make-up,
Trying to make,
Herself beautiful,
For a place,
Or a time,
That seems,
So out of reach,
With red circles,
And haunting blue eyes,
She stares at herself,
In the mirror,
Making promises,
She hopes,
To keep someday,
She stood,
Twirling in her dress,
Barefoot,
She tries to smile,
Seeing herself in the mirror,
Her hair flows,
Like the rain,
Over her shoulders,
It traces her face,

Along a line,
Of beauty.

Dress
A woman,
It defines her,
The way she moves,
Looking into a mirror,
Holding a dress,
One and then another,
Which one,
She dances,
And twirls,
A blue one,
With white flowers,
A red slender one,
She has worn it before,
It hugged her curves,
And matched her lipstick,
She cannot go far these days,
All the places she used to go,
Are a shuttered memory,
To see her friends again,
She holds the dress closer,
Looking at it,
And imagining,
Some guy,
Asking her for a dance,
She mouths the words, "yes,"
As a smile crosses her lips,
There was a time,
When it was a few drinks,

To get her out on the dance floor,
When normal returns,
She would be sober,
So, she could,
Remember every moment,
The way he holds her,
The beat of the song,
Every lyric,
Would become her anthem,
It would be wonderful,
Then reality sets in,
As tears glide down her cheeks,
The dam busts,
And it flows,
It has been years,
Trapped in her house,
She plays dress up,
Alone.

Sister
Mom is gone,
But she left,
Pieces of herself,
In you,
The way you speak,
I hear her voice,
Echo through you,
And when you talk,
With your hands,
When you do,
I find it so difficult,
At times,

To keep a straight face,
Because I don't know,
If I should laugh,
Or cry,
You remind me,
So much of our mom,
I marvel at how much,
You've grown up,
In some ways,
But you're never too old,
To change,
Or to young,
To grow into,
The woman,
Mom wanted you to be,
I'm always here,
For you,
And I will,
Always love you,
Don't give up on your dreams,
Chase after them,
And always create new ones,
But most of all,
Have fun,
And be you.

Streams
It is a wonder,
Sometimes,
People do not know,
How to take me,
When I give them,
My heart?
Or a piece of kindness,

Some people repulse,
At my offer of touch,
They do not know,
My intentions,
When I have nothing,
To hide,
And expect truly,
Little in return,
Because that is all,
I have ever received,
All of my life,
It is something,
I have grown accustom too,
Giving away my heart,
And my love,
Like an ocean,
And gathering,
Small streams in return.

Pillow
Without you,
The bed is colder,
I still feel your ghost,
Lying between the sheets,
Where your form would lay,
Your scent still lingers,
As I hug my pillow close,
Wishing it were you instead,
But it is not enough,
Wanting to feel your touch,
As my body aches,
To feel your presence near me,
Only to no avail,
Your absence is noted,

From our bed,
And my life.

Playing
It is a dance,
The two of us,
Pretend,
As we hide,
Our honesty,
Behind mask,
Isn't it time?
To pull back the veil,
Instead of hiding,
And start being real,
Sharing how we feel,
Rather than lying,
To ourselves,
In how you feel,
About someone,
Who knows,
It might be the best,
Decision,
We have made,
In genuinely,
Loving each other,
Instead,
Of playing games,
Where the rules,
Only make sense to,
The people who fools play.

Damage

Please don't go,
Is there something,
I can say,
To make you stay,
It may be for the best,
But,
You touched my soul,
Did I do the same for you?
Other women don't matter,
Because,
You are the only one, I need,
The one I wanted to feel,
Around me,
Close to me while we slept,
And share my life with,
I guess I should get used to this,
When people leave,
It is not fair,
When you touch my soul,
And just walk away,
Like nothing matters,
Didn't our time together,
Mean something?
Even if it was a moment?
You don't understand the damage,
You have done,
Just by gracing me,
With your presence,
When we kissed,
You left your mark on me,
From your touch,
As you whispered words,
With my heart close to yours,
Feeling how close we were.

Autumn
The leaves are changing,
Giving the days over to winter,
As the leaves fall,
Leaving the trees bare,
Now, only stillness remains,
Before the winds blow,
And the trees,
Start to sing,
Of loneliness,
As the wind howls,
Through the lifeless branches,
And winter,
Holds us in her icy grasp.

Verses
Fumbling over lines,
Trying find something,
That rhymes,
The quill is dry,
Because I spilled the ink,
Such a black mess,
As the lines,
Blur, while others fade,
Traces of ink,
On my fingers,
But blood pours from the tips,
Across the page,
As they mingle,
With the smeared ink,
Into verses,
Phrases cutting into paper,

Of things,
That were a memory,
Forgotten echoes,
Brought about,
By an old song,
Playing a familiar beat,
Of some melancholy,
Daydream,
Of being young,
In love,
Feeling your ghost,
Numb my skin,
From the touch of your hand,
The words,
Flow from my quill,
As I linger,
Here,
Scratching ink,
Of your curves,
Your beauty,
When we kissed,
Under the stars,
Holding hands,
Like I'm holding my pen,
Swaying with the stokes,
Of a brush,
To capture your essence,
In the words,
On an ink blotted page.

Depth
Her voice,

Calms the storms,
Deep within me,
Her light,
Shines,
Chasing away,
The shadows,
Who surround me,
It is all these things,
That makes you beautiful,
Whether you,
Believe me or not,
These are things,
I see of you,
Because I saw your soul,
First and foremost,
Long before I saw your smile,
How your eyes sparkled,
Felt your warm embrace,
And knew the depth of your heart.

Re-quaint
It is an affair of one,
When it's just you,
Holding onto someone,
It does not matter gender,
When it comes to friendships,
Or relationships,
Where one person is giving,
And the other person takes,
Without nothing in return,
Most relationships,
Have percentages,

Beside their names,
As you hold onto hope,
That they would re-quaint you,
With some sort of love,
Or gesture,
Preferably not the finger kind,
But it is an endless circle,
As you love a person,
Who loves someone else,
And they do,
Then don't,
As the circle persist,
Then you wonder,
Why can't you see me?
And waste your energy,
On a person,
Who does not deserve you,
Know how to love you,
Or your love is too pure,
And they do not know,
How to handle your kindness,
So much so it repulses them,
Then again,
They want more of you,
Because you are so easy,
To take advantage of,
So, they eat away at you,
Taking away your energy,
Tapping your love,
Leaving you hurting,
And bleeding on the floor,
As they move,
Onto someone else.

Lines

When we make love,
Which mask,
Do we take off first?
To lay ourselves bare,
Beneath the covers,
And protection of fabric,
In some way,
We find ourselves closer
In a lover's embrace
Before the adrenaline,
Of madness overtakes us,
As we feel its song,
In a moment of passion,
We feel our skin burn,
From our touch,
As we trace the lines,
Of our bodies.

Peak

Creating is like sex,
Where we ride,
The climax of waves,
Between us,
Inspiring each other,
To grow beyond,
Our views,
As our souls fucked,
And the sparks,
Of our embrace,

Fuels our minds,
To find an outlet,
For expression,
As the friction builds,
Between lovers,
Until we reach our peak,
Together as one.

Waves
I enjoy the feeling of you,
The sensation of your touch,
Being close to you,
Not sexual,
But the feel of your energy,
When you are near me,
It gives me comfort,
It is the texture of your skin,
Soft and smooth,
Like waves,
In a puddle,
When you touch her,
And see her reaction,
Just by holding her hand.

Boundaries
I am looking forward,
To the day,
When I find a woman,
Who can give me,
All of her love,
She will not be torn,
Or standing behind boundaries,

We cannot overcome,
That is all I want,
For a woman to love me,
Just as much and deep,
As I love her.

Scraps
Somedays,
She is the only thing I have got,
To get me through,
When you are living off scraps,
Of love or touch,
Just to survive,
And trying to feel human.

Wear
Is a kiss,
Just as intimate,
When done through a mask?
Not the feeling we presume,
Of wanting to be kissed,
The feeling of a first,
After things are done,
And we see each other,
Does absence,
Make the heart grow fonder?
Due to the boundaries,
Set in place,
We can no longer touch,
Kiss or make love,
Without the consequences,
Of getting sick,

So, we wear a veil of protection,
From an unseen enemy,
Our eyes can speak volumes,
Well beyond words,
In expressing feelings,
Sometimes it is a song,
When we can no longer,
Communicate,
Or show our sincerity,
With a smile,
No more kisses,
And touching of skin
Because of the mask we wear,
It hides our frowns and anger,
They go unnoticed,
Where cloth hides our intentions,
So, we must look to the eyes,
The window to the soul,
To tell us the story,
Of pain and sorrow,
When we are distant,
And losing our humanity,
From the lack of contact,
With family or friends,
For the sake of love,
Has rendered us,
Lonely beyond compare,
As we distance ourselves,
From the world around us,
Just to wear a mask.

Whisper
Love doesn't die,
If it does,

It's because we kill it,
And we deliver,
The killing blow,
Love doesn't die,
In violent throws,
Of a fading life,
It's a not a scream,
A cry,
Or a whimper,
But a whisper,
Of what have I done.

Elements

The fire rages,
She reaches out her hand,
As the flames,
Lick at it,
The heat was intense,
As she began to perspire,
The air around her,
Started turning colder,
Her lips,
Spoke above a whisper,
The two elements,
Of fire and ice,
Mingle,
As she raises,
Her other hand,
And throws herself,
Into the flames,
The flames,
Begin to die,
As two figures,

Stand in the fire,
Her embrace,
Shielded him,
From flames,
His will,
Healed her burns,
As they kissed,
The fire burned,
Brighter,
And no longer,
Scorched their flesh.

Palms

Comets streamed,
Through her hair,
As she ran through galaxies,
In her mind,
Reaching out,
With her hands,
Dipping her fingers,
Into the black,
Smudging out stars,
Upon a canvass of smoke,
Stars,
Streamed outwards from her touch,
As planets took shape,
Moons danced,
Beneath her palms,
As she let them go,
Blindly into the night,
Spinning blue tops,
Dazzle,
As she shakes the comets,

From her hair,
As she kisses,
Galaxies into existence,
And blows them about,
For generations,
To explore.

Unfamiliar
It was something,
The way her eyes,
Sparkled,
I took my mask off,
To kiss her lips,
As we hugged each other,
It had been so long,
Since I held her in my arms,
It was for the best I told her,
As days,

Slipped into weeks,
And then months,
When I last held her,
I did it for her,
A woman,
Who was sick,
From an illness,
Brought upon her,
Sometime as a child,
It scarred her,
Leaving her bare,
So, here I am,
Able to hold her,
Once again,
Her body was unfamiliar,

But the ghost of her touch,
Reminded me,
As I kissed her again,
And I fell in love,
Deeper than before,
As we live our lives,
Behind masks.

Uneasiness

What is the reason?
As I stare at my T.V.,
Watching the world,
Falling into chaos,
A sense,
Of uneasiness,
Washes over me,
Followed by despair,
Because all my dreams,
Have died,
In just a matter of moments,
It seems like,
I've lost the chance,
To find love,
Instead,
I'm trapped at home,
Lost,
And sleeping with loneliness,
Sometimes,
My faith feels,
A fist full of sand,
I miss my friends,
And feeling of their embrace,
I feel so cold,
Where only silence,

Is my only friend,
My body aches,
For love,
Or some kind of release,
My sanity is growing thin,
As the days,
Seem to meld into one,
But I sign a death warrant,
Every time,
I step out my door,
For food or gas,
And to go to work,
Work,
That's my only,
Means of social interaction,
Being with people,
Who are essential,
Like lambs to the slaughter,
I feel,
When I deal with,
Being around someone,
Who can expose me,
To an illness,
Modern medicine,
Has no fucking clue about,
So here I sit,
With no means of being social,
When the world,
Is burning.

Games
Even in a fantasy,
I don't get the girl,
That's pretty fucked up,

When the gods of make believe,
Can't bend things in my favor.
In real life,
Women are divided,
When it comes to liking me,
Or there's something,
Keeping them,
From wanting to fall in love,
I get that it could be me,
And I've fought hard to change,
But it just seems,
No matter how hard I try,
Things get out of whack,
And I fall back into,
The downward spiral,
So much so,
I feel myself drowning,
It's mine to despair over it,
I hate being loved by women,
Who are taken,
It just adds to the frustration,
Hearing them say,
If I wasn't married,
I would snatch you up,
In a heartbeat,
Or if I was younger,
We would be dating,
Its these things,
I hear over and over,
Again,
And it crushes me.

Needless
Wrapped up in thorns,

She dances,
Though the needles,
Dig deep into her skin,
She doesn't feel them,
They are a part of her,
As she moves,
They move,
These thorns,
Are her defense,
To keep people at bay,
It's the thing she does,
As she fights to protect herself,
From those who are close to her,
She has no armor,
Only thorns,
Her wounds may bleed,
But she doesn't care,
It's better than a broken heart,
She has come to reason,
Than feeling anything.

Honor
I am your shield,
From the falls of life,
This is my duty,
As a parent,
In showing you,
How to take care of yourself,
So, when you find someone,
You two can work together,
Instead of against each other,
This is why I impressed upon you,
In keeping you safe,

And watching over you,
Long after I'm gone,
I am a piece of you,
You are all of me,
This is a parent's love,
And my honor,
To love you,
And hold you,
No matter how old you are,
You will always be my child.

Canvas
Your body,
Is like a fine wine,
I drink you in,
When I see your silhouette,
Your curves are divine,
Like a painting,
On a canvas,
Your body comes to life.

Filler
I know you,
I felt you,
With every,
Inch of my being,
In loving you,
Before I knew,
The sound,
Of your name,

Being spoken,
Or the taste of it,
On my tongue,
It was like,
A song,
As my mouth,
Said the syllables,
To make,
It just as real,
To me,
As the touch,
Of your skin,
And the warmth,
Of your smile,
When I hold you,
In my arms,
It's so familiar,
The way,
We connect,
Like you're,
The missing piece,
To my life,
And you,
Filled that void.

Wake
Everyone,
Rebels in the storm,
As the fury of the winds,
Leave destruction,
In its wake,
Lightning,
Streaks across,
Clouds,

Breaking the silence,
As the rain falls,
Harder,
Drenching us,
As I kiss you,
Like light rain,
After a thunderstorm.

Wounds
I'm interrupting,
Someone's pain,
So, people who,
Who inflect wounds,
And can't feel,
Will understand,
The pain they cause.
My scars,
Keep me safe,
From the pain,
I share with you,
Because,
I've felt,
Those feelings,
So many times,
Before,
That I am numb,
To the emotions,
The sorrow brings.

Taught
You are,
A fascinating woman,

One of which,
I have,
Never seen before,
It's mesmerizing,
To hear you speak,
Because I find myself,
Captivated,
By your mind,
And the beauty,
Of your soul,
It's how you,
Express yourself,
You are like no-one else,
You have taught me so much,
In how to use my words,
To paint pictures,
Only the mind can see,
And a heart,
Can feel.

Overload
It broke me,
Feeling you,
In my arms again,
Feeling your heartbeat,
Against mine,
As our souls embraced,
They touched,
It sent shock waves,
Through me,
As I laid my head,
Upon your shoulder,
So, I could,
Hold onto you,

Longer,
Tighter,
And never wanting,
To let go of you,
Again,
It hurts,
Being without you,
The touch of you,
Made my senses dance,
It was complete overload,
As you hugged me back,
Your embrace was stronger,
As you squeezed me,
And you whispered,
I'm not letting you go.

Bounce
Rebound,
The roll back,
Of the ball,
As it bounces,
Back to you,
And then to me,
It's an endless cycle,
Where only you know,
When it's going to end,
From me to him,
And then him again,
The way you pivot,
Would make,
A basketball player,
Shatter his ankles,
In trying to guard you,
As you bob and weave,

In not being truthful,
To yourself,
And finding a reason,
To ground yourself,
Instead of moving,
Around the court,
Searching,
For a new dick carousel.

Bloom

This is yours,
It's a piece of me,
I give it freely,
To those I call friend,
It isn't much,
As you can see,
But it is all,
I have to give,
Of me,
While you may not,
See the worth,
Of such a small thing,
Sitting in your palm,
Over time it will grow,
Into something to cherish,
If you help to take care of it,
It's has simple instructions,
You show it kindness,
Love, and respect,
To feed it,
You can water it,
When you share,

Your hopes, dreams,
And aspirations,
And in return,
I will show you mine,
Tell you these feelings,
About my dreams,
And love you,
Like a friend should,
Without judgement,
And accept you,
For you.

Flicker
The flames licked at her skin,
As the drops of water,
Evaporated from its touch,
It was refreshing,
As it flickered,
Concealing her form,
Hiding her parts,
While defining her curves,
As light danced around her,
She felt free,
The smoke rose from her hair,
And sparkled in her eyes.

Bask
Your lips taste like summer
As I draw your scent in,
The scent of honeysuckles,

Lingers in the air,
As we stand close,
Draped all over each other,
Basking in your glow,
The air is cool,
And sweet,
As I taste your lips again.

Falls Apart
I hate doubt
And not knowing,
It feels like,
I'm being punished,
For something,
I didn't do,
Hiding away,
Then doubt sets in,
As my waistline,
Blossoms out,
Getting fatter,
Everything falls apart,
And here I am,
A lonely mess.
Dying alone,
While the world goes on,
What do I do?
I don't want to get caught up,
In the mess of things,
As things fall apart,
The world I once knew,
Is long gone,
And it seems like,
Nothing is going to change,
It's going to last,

For years,
So, all I can look forward too,
Is dying alone,
In place I don't own,
Without anyone,
By my side,
Starving for human touch,
Until I finally give in,
Take my life into my hands,
And search for a woman,
For a one night stand,
To suffer the consequences,
Of wanting a release.

Singer
You feel,
The emotion of a song,
How the pain lingers,
As the singer comes to terms,
With all the hurt inside,
To move on,
When it feels like,
Their world is falling in,
Around them.

Greater
Ignorance attacks,
The weakest link,
Of the chain,
That it's being dangled from,
When someone attacks

Doctors and nurses
For wanting to keep you healthy,
They've been doing this for years,
Only now you rebel,
But it is okay,
To march,
On the steps of a capital,
Like you're going to war,
Just to eat at a restaurant,
Putting yourself in danger,
Or the lives of innocents,
Because bullets are blind,
When misfired,
Due to someone's careless act,
Then it comes down to race,
If someone else,
Of a different color or religion,
Stands in defiance,
They're gunned down,
Or held down,
Until they can't breathe
Because they're a terrorist,
Or maybe in the wrong place,
At the wrong time,
Due to the color of their skin,
And you violate their rights,
Spin it how you want,
When idiots are in control,
Sipping their bleach cocktail,
I can tell you now,
It doesn't matter,
Gender,
Race,

Or station,
The people you think,
Support you,
Because you cast your vote,
To make a nation great,
Don't even know your name,
If someone is deciding,
Based on money,
Greed is king,
And were all paupers.
Gather up all your memories,
Of the places you once knew,
Because the slate,
Is going to be wiped clean,
Your family and friends,
Will be gone,
And all that remains,
Will be the memory of them,
As people let greed,
Drive their decisions,
For the power of a dollar,
When debts should be forgiven,
Instead of being paid in blood,
Of innocent lives.

Bring Myself
I can't explain,
How we've never hugged,
I guess having a crush on you,
And past failures,
Rendered me touch-less,
Whenever I am near you,
Where the thought makes me,

Self-aware of you,
And how much I want you,
But I can't bring myself,
To ask you,
For human emotion,
And feel your body,
Next to mine.

The Escape
The morning mist rises,
From the dew,
Carefully placed,
On each blade of grass,
Birds sing,
Their morning song,
Welcoming the sun,
The beautiful and majestic,
Horses galloping in the grass,
In my neighbor's yard,
The fence is down,
And they are free,
For greener pastures they roam,
Much to my dismay,
With feed bucket in hand.
And a bridal in the other,
I wonder into the rising sun,
To fetch my horses,
From their brief,
Fling with freedom.

Heart Of A Man
I am here,

You and I,
Walk together,
Do you remember?
When I carried you?
I do,
Wiped your tears,
Held your hand,
Or Listened,
When it seemed like,
No one else,
Would understand,
I did,
Your laughter,
Made my heart sing,
Because you are a part of me,
I want to tell you,
I am not gone,
You will hear my voice,
Feel my touch,
Know my laugh,
Because I am in you,
There is a piece,
Of me within you,
Guiding you,
Just look in the mirror,
I am there,
Smile, it's me,
Laugh, can you hear me?
I will be with you,
Always.

Feeling Human
Have you thought,

About touch?
And the power,
You hold within your hands?
Touch calms,
The storms of stress,
It lowers the heart rate,
And relieves blood pressure,
Strengthens immunity,
And helps,
Working memory,
This is why touch,
Is so important,
It communicates,
Your feelings,
To people that you love,
Just as words,
Paint pictures of love,
Touch fills in the gaps,
Where words,
Lose their meaning,
Feeling the lack of touch,
Can send people,
Into depression,
But the sensation of you,
Is all a person needs?
To feel human again.

Here
I am safe,
Warm,
Drifting away,
As my mind,

Subsides,
The feeling,
Of you,
As I lay my head,
On your chest,
Your arms,
Wrapped around me,
Listening to your,
Heartbeat,
Beneath me,
The rhythm,
Of you,
Is soothing,
Stroking your skin,
With my fingers,
As your hand,
Rubs my back,
This is what I missed,
Home,
In a place,
Where I can be,
Human,
And only,
You,
Can see,
This side of me,
Deep down,
We trust,
Each other,
As we lie,
Bonded together,
As our fingers,
Intertwine,
Our souls,
Exchange stardust,
And memories,

Of times together,
As we write,
Our won future.

Empathy
You don't,
Know the feeling,
Of chaos,
Watching,
People you love,
Fall apart,
And being ripped,
Asunder,
By the forces of life.

It's
Your breath,
Is life,
And it beats.

Intend
I read your words,
Because they're,
An extension of you,
Every syllable,
And its meaning,
To me as you,
Say or type them,
Echo,

From your soul to mine,
Sometimes things,
Get lost in the translation,
But I don't intend,
For these assumptions,
To be made between us,
Those words,
I hear or read,
Are like you,
Expressing your soul,
To me,
Laying yourself bare,
Where I feel you,
In so many ways,
Almost to the point,
Where your words,
Create images,
Of the things,
That bring you joy,
So, I know,
Every emotion,
When you're hurting,
Happy,
Excited,
Anxious,
Or angry,
It speaks volumes,
Before it leaves your lips,
I feel that energy,
Like a tidal wave,
And there are days,
Where I drown in you.

◆ ◆ ◆

The poem below was published in Poet Speak Magazine issue #34.

Rhythms

I know hugging you,
Feels like breathing,
For the first time,
After holding my breath.
I thirst for you.
Your embrace,
Is like heaven,
On Earth,
The cool of rain,
Warmth of the sun,
And calm of a gentle breeze,
As we touch,
And our souls align,
Our hearts mend,
As they beat together,
Matching rhythms,
As our heart strings intertwine.

◆ ◆ ◆

Know Me

Before you love me,
You have to know,
That I am flawed,
But I am a diamond,
If you ever,
Give me a chance,
No, I'm not rich,
These good looks will fade,
My clothes are tattered,
And sometimes,

My strength fails me,
However,
I will love you,
So long,
As my mind is strong,
My heart will always,
Be yours,
I will hold you,
Make love to you,
All I ask of you,
In return,
Is to love me,
The same way,
I love you,
Become,
A reflection of love,
For me.

Of Forever

When you want someone,
To be the meaning,
Of forever,
But you don't know,
How to find a way,
To bring her alive.
Even though you know,
She is there watching,
And all you want,
Is to let her hold you.

Those Flames

You're an angel,

You're not perfect,
No one is,
When I look,
Into your eyes,
I saw your spark,
Deep within your soul,
And I wanted,
To fan those flames,
Not only of desire,
But for you to believe,
In yourself again,
And love yourself,
Even more,
To see yourself,
As you're meant to be,
Loved.

Brotherhood
There's a situation brewing
And people are drawing lines,
Taking sides when they should,
Stand together,
But why is hate so strong?
Because it's fueled by ignorance,
Due to the color of someone's skin,
We're all the same,
With crimson beneath our flesh,
We all have minds,
But things stagnate us,
It doesn't have to be this way,
It's bad enough we break each other down,
Instead of building one and another up,
We destroy their foundations,
And knock them off their game,

Because we can't get pass the success of others,
Why is this the norm?
For all of us,
We have the potential,
To be so much more,
When we stand side-by-side,
So, we can unite,
And show people,
The meaning of brotherhood.

❖ ❖ ❖

The poem below was published in Issue
#34 of Poet Speak Magazine.

Desire
Is painful,
The ache is unbearable,
When you're wanting,
To feel someone,
Close to you at night,
Legs entwined,
Feeling another human being,
Lying next to you,
The frustration,
Mounts with each passing day,
As you grow numb,
And want to sleep away,
The sadness,
Of being alone,
In an empty house.

Except
You know,

You've come to the end,
When your frustrated,
About things
That are beyond your control,
When wanting something,
And there's nothing you can do,
Except let go.

◆ ◆ ◆

Dry
It's like dying,
Only you survive it,
Just to witness,
Your heart being torn out,
Over-and-over again,
There's nothing you can do,
Just sit back,
And watch things burn,
You don't know how to cope,
With things going on,
Now, you're stuck,
Being alone,
And going crazy,
Because all the opportunities,
You once had,
Dried up,
And blown away,
So, here I sit,
In a huddled mess,
Needing someone's touch,
With some love thrown in,
Maybe a little sex,
Just to feel,
Like I am human again,
And feel your skin,

Pressed again mine,
Tasting your lips.

Atone
How much longer,
Must I atone,
For the sins of my past,
I was young,
And wanting something,
Which eluded me,
It seems,
Like all my sins,
Come bubbling up,
I thought I had moved,
Past those mistakes,
Learned from them,
But something,
Keeps wanting me,
To play them over,
Repeating them,
Even though,
I had managed,
To correct myself,
And forgiven me,
And others,
I can't break free,
Of the chains that bind me,
So, I'm a slave to my desires.

Dealing
There are days,
When I hate my life,

And dealing with people,
Due to the way that I am,
It's so frustrating,
Wanting something,
Other people,
Have no problem,
In getting or taking,
I feel like I'm starving,
And there's nothing to eat,
When it comes to human touch,
Or sex,
What is wrong with me?
And what does it take,
To finally feel some kind,
Of release,
To be human.

◆ ◆ ◆

Sloping Away
There's so little to dream,
As things,
Feel like their slipping away,
And all you can do,
Is struggle,
To tighten your grip,
In vain,
As things slip,
Through your fingers,
So, you cup your hands,
To slow the fall,
Of the sands,
Emptying from the hourglass.

◆ ◆ ◆

Elementals
The soul,
Is made of,
The of the elements,
Of stars,
And planets,
From times,
Long ago,
Where lights mingle,
Among the heavens,
Only to fall to Earth,
Where they're born,
Live, and die,
While searching,
For a piece,
Of their souls,
So, they can,
Return to the elements,
From which,
They were born.

Holding Heaven
Deep,
Is where,
I am,
Lost,
In your eyes,
Your smile,
And your touch,
It is like holding heaven,
In these arms.

Your Eyes
Speak volumes,
More than words,
Could ever mean,
It was like,
You came alive,
When I spoke to you,
And feeling,
Your touch,
Made the pain,
Go away,
As I read you,
These words,
My heart spoke to you,
Whispering a song,
Of wanting to touch,
Your soul again,
And feeling the warmth,
Of holding an angel,
In my arms,
While loving you,
With all that I am.

Ashes
She is fire,
It drips,
From her soul,
Like rain,
Pouring from the clouds,
That she,
Burns away,
Her sadness,
And turns,

Madness,
Into ashes.

Bad Idea
I burn,
All over,
The fever,
Is breaking,
Upon me,
This,
Was a bad idea,
Being close,
To you,
I just want to hide,
Sleep,
Somehow,
Step away,
I can feel it,
Beneath my skin,
Boiling,
Like a raging sea,
There's nothing,
I can do,
But melt,
Over,
And over,
Again,
As it singes,
The hairs on my body,
And feeling your touch,
Only draws,
The poison deeper,
Into me,
As my madness,

Rises,
Like a tide,
That drowns me,
Suffocates me,
As I try,
To hide my ache,
Away.

Shifting
Trying to hold,
Myself together,
And keep,
From falling apart,
These emotions,
Are draining.

Twin
We're pieces,
Two souls,
It seems like,
I could be wrong,
But I miss,
Feeling you,
Your touch,
Awakens me,
But it kills me,
As I try to hold on.

◆ ◆ ◆

Distinct
Something new,

When I spoke to you,
Your eyes,
Took on a distinct color,
A different tone,
As I looked into them,
I saw the jewel,
Of your soul,
As you smiled,
It was unique,
Seeing beyond the fire,
Pass the sparks,
To the embers,
Of you,
I wanted to touch you,
While I tasted your lips,
And felt your heart beating,
Next to mine,
Being held by you.

Feel you
How can I describe,
Being held by you,
It's like heaven,
If that is what it is like,
Your soft,
Smooth,
Satin or silk,
To my touch,
As I feel you.

A Way
I want to tell you,

Thank you for being you,
I enjoy talking to you,
And hearing your voice.
It is amazing,
Sometimes how much power,
You have in the words you speak.
You calm the storms within me,
There are times,
Where I wish,
I could find a way to calm yours.

Sublime
I just want to feel,
The memory of touch,
Something surreal,
Would be sublime,
I can't recall,
The touch of your skin,
Feeling your embrace,
A memory of how our eyes met,
I've forgotten,
And all I feel now,
Is my own numb skin.

Burning Inside
I'm not sorry,
For how I feel,
When my body,
Betrays me
For all the things,
I feel,
I'm burning inside,

People think I'm desperate,
When all I want,
Is to feel something real,
I'm tired of dying inside,
And try to hide my rage,
When I want to feel,
The touch of another human,
I'm so desperate for something,
And the feeling of a release,
I'm tired of feeling the same,
Because people I know,
Laugh at me,
All the time,
And I'm tired of feeling ashamed,
For wanting something more,
When a friend can grant me mercy.

Dances
They call it desperation,
Yet, I don't think,
That it is the same,
If I would have known the outcome,
Of the things to come,
I would have thrown it all away,
Instead of being a gentleman,
In needing a release,
I regret not doing more,
In putting myself out there,
And writing hardcore,
Seeing how things,
Are going,
When you want so much more,
And you can't feel anything,
Because you're numb from the pain,

I just want to understand,
How come,
Everything just fades,
Into a memory,
The way I feel,
That I've got to deal,
With it every day,
It makes no sense,
The desperation I feel,
I'm not sorry it,
I just want a woman,
Just for a minute or two,
That's probably how long I'll last,
Given how long it's been,
I would have thrown it all away,
In kicking the gentleman in me,
To the curb,
If I would have known about this virus,
I wouldn't have squandering my chances,
Leaving those dances.

Real Me
This is the real me,
It's not depression,
I just wanted to say,
I'm going crazy,
Just wanting to feel something,
More than emptiness,
I want to drink you in,
And let you become my drug,
As I get high off of you,
So, somehow,
I can feel again,
And keep from being numb,

I feel like I'm on the verge,
Feeling the stress building within
And no matter what I do,
I can't find a way to deal,
With all the pain,
I feel it,
It's creeping up inside me,
I'm about to explode,
In wanting to feel the touch of a woman,
I cry so much more,
I tell you it's my addiction,
As I let my body drink in your touch,
I want to explore you,
For more than just a feeling of you,
Because it drives me insane
I know this is desperation,
I've lost too much of myself,
When I gave it all away,
Just be human,
And call it a day.

Divine Way
I admire you,
You're everything,
I would want in a woman,
In a companion,
Loving touch,
Kind hugs,
The way our fingers,
Entwine,
When I look into your eyes,
I've never seen,
Anything like them,
And I don't know why,

I find myself,
So, mesmerized,
By them,
You feel so soft,
Under the touch,
Of my hands,
And your warm embrace,
Makes me want to cling,
Closer to you,
I can only imagine,
What it would be like,
To love someone like you,
Only to feel their love,
In return,
Without boundaries,
And nothing standing,
Between us,
Where we are free,
To fall in love,
And explore each other,
Being transparent,
In our relationship,
All the while,
Making love,
On a deeper level,
So, much more than skin,
Beyond the elements,
And stardust,
Lurking beneath our breath,
To our souls,
As they call each other,
By their ancient names,
As they love,
In a divine way.

Caretaker
A woman,
Being, of grand design,
In elegance,
And beauty,
Isn't defined,
By status,
Only truth,
Compassion,
And kindness,
But she has armor,
Made of steel,
Binding her skin,
She is vulnerable,
And human,
Like so many angels,
Who cares for the lost,
Forgotten,
And castaways,
Of life,
Because she knows,
Just how precious,
Life can be.

Pertained
These are my words,
I speak to you,
They may not be eloquent,
Send shivers down your spine,
Give you goosebumps,
Or make you feel the kiss,
Of a gentle lover,
They may not wrap you up,

And protect you,
They might take away your fears,
Guide you,
Or help you understand,
How truly special you are,
But these words I speak,
The fumbling madness,
Pertained in the syllables,
As I speak your name,
With love on my mind,
Is the only way,
I can touch you,
When we're not together.

Tucking Away
Touching you,
I do that slowly,
Drawing you in,
Like a breath,
To where you stop,
When our bodies touch,
There's a reason for this,
Due to the way things are,
I want to remember,
The feel of you,
As I hold you,
Marking where bare skin touches,
Feeling your energy,
As I hold onto you,
Remembering it,
Tucking away your touch,
To console me,
When you and I can't,
And no one else is around,

So, I'll have something,
To remember you by,
Until I'm able to hold you again,
Hopefully longer,
And never let you go.

◆ ◆ ◆

Expression
Little shards,
Of dancing joy,
It's a melancholy feeling,
Expressing something,
You feel deep inside,
That you can't share,
With people,
And you can't begin,
To understand how,
To explain these feelings,
When you're so confused,
About what you truly desire,
Holding someone,
With the right person,
Will last as they lay,
Beside you,
Being intimate in that way,
Wanting sex,
Means that this person,
Will not be around long enough,
To relieve the ache,
Of wanting,
To feel another person,
Wrapped up in your arms.

◆ ◆ ◆

Headlong

There are times,
When I wonder.
Why I suffer like this,
There are so many,
Easier ways than this,
As I tend to rush,
Headlong into things,
Where my heart and mind,
Are wondering,
What the fuck am I doing,
By letting people,
Get close to me,
Only to have them leave,
It was so frustrating,
In dealing with things,
But I wonder now,
If everything that happened,
Was away to prepare me,
For the months of isolation,
It still sucks,
When you want,
To be close to someone,
Breathe their breath,
As they lay close to you,
Maybe naked or clothed,
Either way,
Just being wrapped up,
In the arms of a woman,
Whether in lustful throws,
Or feeling the compassion,
Of a long embracing hug.

Beings
Your light,
Shines brighter,
Than the stars,
In a someone's darkness,
Because you,
Radiant the sun,
At its most hottest point,
And you pull me in,
With the gravity,
Of your kiss,
And the sensual,
Being that you are.

Tears
Are clear,
But they carry,
Burdens,
Of pain,
Heartache,
Lost love,
Frustration,
And fear,
Sometimes,
They build strength,
Define character,
And joy,
Laughter too,
It's amazing,
Something so small,
Can wash away,
Hurt.

Give
I don't know,
What to do,
When you,
Want something,
That is so innocent,
And people,
Just walk away,
It's strange,
When they,
Give themselves,
So freely to others,
But someone is on fire,
They wouldn't spare,
A drop of water,
To quench my flames,
Why is that?
They waste,
Their time on fools,
Only to piss away things,
With those,
Who wouldn't care for them.

Unfilled
I wish,
I could find,
Something real,
Something more,
Then the touch,
Of a fantasy.

Madman's Spark
Lost in thought,
Between fantasy,
A daydream,
And reality,
I wonder,
What bridges,
Did I burn,
Without realizing,
The match,
Had been struck,
It doesn't bother me,
One less person,
I have to deal with,
But I still yearn,
To feel something real,
Instead of chasing,
After a fantasy,
That can't be fulfilled,
There aren't any loopholes,
In wanting something more,
Unless I want,
To remain here,
And go insane,
So, what do I do?
In searching,
For a woman,
To quench the fires,
That burn in me,
Or does a person,
Like this,
Truly exist,
For a madman,
Like me.

◆ ◆ ◆

Joke
It was the way,
We made love,
That still haunts me,
The way I felt,
After you said,
I wasn't enough,
To quench your desire,
By telling me,
You had better,
When we finished,
Making love,
There was no jokes,
Only silence,
As your words,
Cut me to my core,
Even though,
I gave you,
All of me,
It didn't matter,
To someone like you.

Power
I often wonder,
What it would be like,
Making love to an angel,
It might be like,
Touching the divine,
Angels are known,
For their power,
And you,

Render me,
Powerless,
With just a glance,
Would your curves,
Be the same,
Like a mortal woman.

Through the Flames
Just so you know,
Angels,
Who are born of fire,
Can walk through,
The flames,
And never be touched,
You are one,
Of those angels,
Who has walked,
Through life,
Gathering your scars,
So, one day,
You can defend those,
Who have lost their way.

❖ ❖ ❖

Magical Storm
There's magic,
In the storm of her,
Not in chaos,
Where other women,
Are known,
To desire,
But the calm,
Of whom she is,

In the way,
She finds,
Balance there,
The way things,
Are meant to be,
For a woman,
Of magic.

Push
You're perfect,
I think,
You should know,
Due to your presence,
Here in my life,
You help me to smile,
When I am sad,
Lonely or melancholy,
You know what buttons,
To push to get,
Through to me,
And a lot of times,
I didn't know,
Those were there,
Or forgotten,
The meaning of their use,
It was either by,
The touch,
Of your hand,
Or the way,
Your body felt,
Against mine,
Where I felt alive,
For a brief moment,
And I wanted,

To linger there,
Because it felt,
So much like home,
I didn't want to leave.

Pull
Your gravity,
Is strong,
As you,
Pull me into you,
It's your love,
And you,
Have me,
In your grasp,
As we orbit,
Each other,
Like to stars,
Sharing light,
As we are locked,
In a gaze,
Pulling towards you,
And you me,
My light,
Becomes yours,
Yours,
Mine,
Burning brighter,
And hotter,
With each,
Revolution,
We turn,
As we collide,
Creating life.

◆ ◆ ◆

Refuge
The eyes of a woman,
Are soft and sensual,
They are a place,
Of refuge,
When you gaze into them,
There you will find bliss,
Of a halo of colors,
Like a prism,
Where beauty,
Resides,
In sparkling brilliance,
I want to get lost there,
Looking into a place,
Where your soul shines,
I would spend hours,
Just holding you,
While gazing,
Into happiness,
Just to watch,
As they sparkle,
With delight,
Maybe I'll see heaven there,
Or vast galaxies,
Where stars are born,
As you whisper them,
Into being,
I would be so inclined,
To fall into you,
Over and over again,
Drifting upon a sea,
Of stardust,
In your soul,

As I forget myself,
And kiss your lips,
Just for a moment,
To know what it is like,
In kissing an angel.

Whatever
It's like,
A never-ending tide,
Trying to drown you,
When you turn,
On the news,
And something,
Else in the world,
Has completely,
Blown a gasket,
Or somehow,
The virus,
Has changed,
In some way,
All you can do,
Is shake your head,
As you try to hold,
Onto what is left,
To the frayed,
Pieces of your sanity,
You want to cry,
And sometimes you do,
Staining your pillow,
As the only freedom,
You have is going to work,
Wrapped up in a mask,
To keep from catching,
Something,

From a weekend bender,
Or a night of surrender,
In being an animal,
Then the lines,
Become blurred,
As people talk about skin,
And throw,
In a selfish phrase,
When people are dying,
Because being black,
Means you have a target,
Always on your back,
When someone in blue,
Is messing with you,
It's so much worse,
For black people today,
They fear for their lives,
Because the ones,
Who pull the trigger,
Are labelled brothers and sisters,
Then,
To make matters worse,
If losing lives,
Wasn't bad enough,
You have people,
Choosing sides,
Over wearing masks,
People partying,
Which I wouldn't mind,
A party myself,
Where I'm able to feel,
The touch of a woman,
And making love to her,
To be honest,
It better be,
The best sex ever,

If I'm risking my life,
In breaking off,
A piece of bliss.

Life Fades
The frustration,
Weighs me down,
Of seeing things,
That make you reticent,
About what,
Your future holds,
Because you watch it,
Slowly burn away,
Piece-by-piece,
Ember-to-ember,
As ashes form,
You just watch helpless,
As you blow the ashes,
Away with your breath,
Playing with the flames,
And you're,
No longer concerned,
About being burned,
Since you are numb,
To everything around you,
The fire glows,
Flickers,
Dances,
Being mesmerized,
By all that once was,
As life fades into memory,
Dreams waste away,
Hope dies,
But the fire burns,

Even when your tears,
Touch the flames.

Curled
I wish you were here,
As we lay together,
Curled up,
Just so I could,
Feel you,
Next to me,
In the darkness,
Of my room,
Holding hands,
While saying nothing,
As our hands touch,
Drifting off to sleep.

Recounting
There's a connection,
Between us,
Of stardust,
Where supernovas,
Spring to life,
As we touch,
When we lace fingers,
Contact is made,
As we draw each other,
In for a hug,
We swap our core,
As our hearts beat,
Together in rhythm,
Cradling you,

In my arms,
Holding hands,
While we close our eyes,
As our energy,
Vibes between us,
Recounting,
Your touch,
As I yearn,
To hold you closer,
And feel your kiss,
From the connection,
We made.

Swapping Pieces
I want,
To lie helpless,
In your arms,
As I hold,
Onto you,
Bend all the rules,
Just to look,
Deeply into,
Your eyes,
As you,
Touch my face,
I want to,
Pass the time away,
With you,
Go nowhere,
Or be somewhere,
With you,
We touch,
Our foreheads,
Together,

Letting our minds,
Feel our thoughts,
As my hand,
Follows,
Along your back,
In wanting,
To trace you,
Beneath your skin,
As we embrace,
Letting our hearts,
Speak to each other,
As they mend,
Their broken shards,
Swapping pieces,
As they beat,
Our souls connect,
When our fingers,
Intertwine,
Into knots,
While our bodies,
Feel the passion,
Building,
In places,
Where stars are formed,
It just between us,
In this moment,
Wrapped up,
In your arms,
Our love,
Blooms.

Above All
A friend,
Like you,

Is so rare,
You are priceless,
In who you are,
And so valuable,
Like a breath,
There are so many,
Parts to who you are,
An angel,
Who shelters,
Those you love,
And protect,
But above all else,
It's your heart,
That sets you apart,
From everyone else.

Kittens
It's all about,
Perspective,
If you will,
Lose weight,
And people,
Are all over it,
Wanting to know,
What you did,
How you managed it,
Lose your mine,
And people flee,
They don't want to know,
Because,
You unsettle,
The balance,
Within them,
In having to deal,

With things,
Around them,
They live the lie,
Of things are fine,
Sipping their wine,
Not realizing,
They're closer,
To the edge,
Then you were,
When you flipped,
Your shit,
And delivered a response,
To all the bullshit,
People want to peddle,
Or push,
The dumpster fire is lit,
It's been burning,
Out of control,
And no one wants,
To put out the fire,
As it spreads,
Taking over everything,
And here's the reason,
People are complicated,
And no one,
Wants to spend time,
Getting to know people,
On a deeper level,
It's safer not knowing,
That the person,
You've been friends with,
Who deals with demons,
That would make yours,
Look like drunk kittens.

Unknown
So much is happening,
And no one knows,
How to handle things,
All they want to do is rage,
And push back against things,
All lives matter,
Nope, Black lives matter,
They're the only ones,
Who walk out their door,
Every day with a target,
Painted on their backs,
The only difference is,
It's their own brothers and sisters,
Who can pull the trigger too,
All those who preach hate,
Toward their fellow man,
Can suck it.

Regretful Choices
I hate a lot of things,
But the fact of the matter,
I don't want to die,
I'll wear my mask,
Social distance,
And do my best to stay sane,
Which I dance on the edge,
Every day,
In trying to cope,
Being lonely and living,
With regret,
From all the choices,
I made up to now,

In not doing more,
And wanting,
This to be over,
So, I can pick up,
Where I left off,
Instead,
Of wasting time.

Trading Parts
I'll trade you this,
For that,
Maybe that one,
For this one,
This would look,
So much better on you,
Swapping out,
Old for new to you,
One piece,
For another.
Building,
You into the person,
You should be,
As I trade pieces,
Of myself for you.

String Along
I don't want,
To feel anymore,
I want to be numb,
I don't want,
To deal with things,
I just want,

To push it all away,
Not think of you,
Dream of you,
Or fantasize,
About someone,
I can't have,
The pain is too great,
For me to take anymore,
Being alone here,
Makes it harder,
To string along the days,
Of being without,
When you love someone,
And all you do,
Is grasp for a fantasy,
When you yearn,
To be with someone,
Who is out of reach.

Rain or Shine
You can,
Visualize things,
Sunshine or rain,
Whether you have light,
To see your troubles,
As they come,
Or you can watch,
Them, float away,
From all the heavy rain,
In your life,
It's a matter of opinion,
And perspective,
Rain helps things grow,
Too much,

And it drowns,
Sun helps things grow too,
Too much,
And things wilt,
Dry out.,
The right combination,
And life is renewed,
So, find your balance.

Disconnect
Maybe silence,
Isn't a bad thing,
And finding a way,
To be grounded,
When you want,
A trivial existence,
But you lack,
The things to make it so,
All the pieces don't connect,
Or fall into place.

Delicate
Your skin,
Is like satin,
Like the delicate,
Petal of a rose,
Holding your beauty,
In the palm of my hands,
Kissing you softly,
Slowly,
Drifting along,
Your body,
Taking you in,
Trying to make,

Love to you,
While making,
Our moment together,
Last longer,
Than a faded memory,
Of the time,
I caressed,
The heart of an angel,
With my feeble hands.

Awakening
It had been awhile,
Since I felt your touch,
It was something,
My body craved,
And like,
An old memory,
My heart,
Remembered you,
And the feeling,
Of your touch,
It awoke old feelings,
Memories,
And the desire,
Of wanting you,
In feeling your touch,
When we hugged.

Wash
I desire you,
Like a breath,
So, you can quench,

My thirst of your touch,
As I feel you,
With every inch,
Of my being,
Like feeling rain,
Washing over me,
The way your kisses do,
When we're alone,
As I hold you,
For longer,
Than a moment.

Original Delight
Your touch,
Is intoxicating,
Like a bottle of Jack,
Smooth, and sweet.
On the tongue,
My head is in a swirl,
When I hold your hand,
Our fingers,
Lazily intertwined.
I can hear you breathing,
As I hold you in my arms,
Lying under the sheets,
Your body rises and falls,
With every breath,
Your hair is a mess,
Rolling over your body,
Spreading out,
Like the waves,
Crashing upon the shore,
Your skin,
Glistens in the light,

Tiny beads of delight,
Drape across your chest.
The smell of roses,
Fills the air,
Candles flames burn,
As shadows,
Dance along the walls,
I trace your face with my hand,
Soft as velvet,
You nuzzle closer to me,
Our eyes meet,
We kiss,
Short, sweet and sensual.
Your eyes,
Sparkle in the candlelight,
Our bodies cooling,
From the marathon,
Of sex and comfort,
A roller-coaster,
Of positions, and triangles,
It was a dance,
Of two souls finding peace,
That human touch,
Finding a release.
I awake from my dream,
The room is still, empty
And I am alone,
I got to pee.

Slipping Away
It was you,
All along,
The one,
I had,

Been,
Searching for,
As I finally,
Hold you,
In my arms,
Your eyes,
Are beautiful,
Much like,
Your mothers',
I can see myself,
In your face,
Your smile is mine,
You're all,
I've ever wanted,
As you,
Hold my finger,
With your hand,
You glide off to sleep,
As I sway,
Holding you,
In my arms,
As a dream,
Slips way.

Imagining
What would it be like,
To hold you,
Instead of holding,
Onto someone else?
Feeling you hug me,
Before I ask,
Knowing your name,
And how eloquent,
It sounds,

In finding,
The meaning of you,
I want to learn,
The mystery of you,
While touching your face,
So, I know you are real,
And feel your love for me,
Rather than imagining what,
It would be like.

Beneath it All
Courage,
What is it?
Is it storming the beaches,
Pulling someone from the flames,
Shielding someone,
Yes, it is a lot of those things,
But courage,
Is finding the strength,
To get up and shower,
After breaking up,
And mourning the passing,
Of a relationship,
After two years,
Being so close,
To becoming a dad,
Where the strings were cut,
So, you go about your life,
Trying to heal yourself,
Moving on,
For a better tomorrow,
Then you lose,
Your mom,
And everything you knew,

Comes crashing down,
Around you,
There's no ache in the world,
That can compare to losing,
A parent,
Nothing comes close,
So, you struggle,
Putting together days,
In being brave,
Because so much more,
Rests on your shoulders,
In taking things
One moment at a time,
And fight,
Not to fall back,
Into the hole,
You once filled,
By being stuck,
To overcome things,
That would have,
Made other people,
Cry from the pain,
So, you grow,
You learn,
You heal yourself,
Find pieces of you,
That were scattered,
Like wreckage,
Strummed along,
The many lives,
Of people you once were,
Until one day,
You stand looking in the mirror,
Staring at the reflection of man,
Who's walked through hell,
Chipping away,

At the blacken flesh,
To reveal,
A new human beneath it all.

Fire Goddess
You spend so long,
Looking for something,
In the way of love,
Not the feeling of sex,
Just the expression of love,
It comes in many forms,
In more ways,
Then people can ponder,
As you lay,
Lazily,
In the arms,
Of a beauty,
Hugging her curves,
While feeling her skin,
Beneath your fingertips,
Smooth as silk,
And soft as rose petals,
Her gentle touch,
Is like heaven,
As your worries,
Drift away,
Where calm,
And peace,
Have full reign,
Lying in the arms,
Of a fire goddess,
As she shelters you,
With her warmth,
Letting you dream,

Of peace.

Vibrations
Your beauty,
Is visually stunning,
It's like seeing,
A setting sun,
For the first time,
Or hearing a song,
Where the melody,
Strikes a familiar chord,
Like touching the surface,
Of a lake,
And watching the ripples,
Dance out across,
The water,
This is how I feel,
Every time,
I touch you,
Sensing the waves,
Of vibrations,
Between us,
When we hug,
We hold hands,
Or lazily touch,
My neck,
I can see those,
Strings,
Attached to you and me,
Along the kindness,
Of the feeling,
When you strum,
My heart chords,
When you return,

My touch.

Freefalling
I would make,
Love to you,
In a heartbeat,
Just to taste,
Your lips,
No hesitation,
As I gather you,
In my arms,
Just to feel you.

Tell You
How can I tell you,
You're beautiful?
Maybe it's the way,
Your eyes look,
When I find myself,
Lost in them,
Even in my dreams,
I'm spellbound,
By you,
It's definitely,
Your smile for sure,
Even when you are down,
There is a slight,
Grin beneath the glum,
I would be lying,
If I didn't say your body,
Was a close in the race,
You're the first real,

Person,
I was able to hold,
And not feel like,
I was imagining things,
While dreaming,
Clutching a pillow,
Wishing to be held,
By someone,
With a pulse,
Your mind,
And how you,
Contemplate things,
Or how it works,
Because I am in awe,
Of you a person,
I love how your eyes,
Light up,
Followed by your face,
When you,
Think of something,
Divine or naughty,
The naughty,
Is the most exciting,
Because you are a woman,
You are so beautiful,
The way your clothes,
Hug your curves,
The touch of your hand,
Sends my body,
Into confusion,
Whether it wants,
To lie helpless,
Letting your touch,
Take away my sorrows,
Or make love to a graceful,
Beauty of a goddess,

Just to taste your kisses,
And feel you beneath me,
As we follow in sync,
To the rhythm,
Of our bodies delight.

Wanting
Have you wanted,
Something,
So bad,
But no matter,
How hard you try,
It seems,
Completely out of reach,
When you want a woman,
Not for sex,
But a companion,
And a lover,
Some feel,
There's no difference,
And there is,
When you feel the touch,
Of another human,
More than anything,
Only you have to make due,
On the generosity of friends,
It stings,
But when it's what you need,
More than what you want,
Is the keystone,
In finding your balance,
You trust,
Those around you,
Love them,

And hope someday,
You will find someone,
Who will encompass,
Them all,
And love you,
With all their might,
So, your scars heal,
Mend your trust.

Attached
What would,
It be like,
To hold you,
Without any,
Strings attached,
Without worry,
Of whom your heart,
Belongs too,
Just two people,
Making a connection,
It's a dream,
Silly as it may seem,
Imaging you,
Would it be bliss,
Clinging to you,
As you held me.

Connect
You made,
It possible,
To feel again,
In knowing,

What it is like,
Holding a person,
It is grand,
Knowing,
This is what,
It means,
Being human,
Making a connection,
With someone,
It was the things,
Or feeling,
My body,
Had craved,
And it hungered,
For it.

Sunburn
I love your curves,
And tracing your beauty,
Along your lines,
Of your silhouette,
My fingers burn,
Touching the skin,
Of the fire goddess,
While basking,
In your glow.

Karma
Thank you,
For walking away,
If it wasn't for you,
I would have never,

Found myself,
Been brave,
Lived with regret,
And accomplished,
Somethings,
For this I thank you,
I didn't understand,
At first,
But now I do,
It was all planned out,
For me to have,
Something greater,
Then you,
So, you made me into,
A better person,
When you destroyed me.

Wonderful
I often wonder,
What are you,
Thinking about,
Looking into,
Your eyes,
Pale blue,
Much like mine,
And so much,
Like your mother,
When you smile,
I guess you,
And I,
Are lost,
In each other's gaze,
My little girl,
I wonder,

What great things,
Will you do,
With your life,
Even if you,
Barely change,
The world,
I will always,
Cheer you,
You're amazing,
My little one,
Here as I rock you,
Swaying together,
You are mesmerizing,
Even as you sleep,
Such a tired,
Little girl,
With blue eyes,
What a wonder,
The world,
Must be to you,
Everything,
Is so new,
Just as you are,
To me.

Thrill Ride
I've tried,
Fantasizing,
About you,
It's hard for me,
To imagine,
What it would be like,
Having sex with you,
Would it be,

A roller coaster,
Thrill ride,
An elegant dance,
Of fire and passion,
Or the kind of sex,
Where you feel,
Heaven on Earth.

Zoned Out
When a woman,
Says you're sweet,
Does nothing,
For you,
You've been placed,
Officially in the zone,
It's just her way,
Of saying to you,
Fuck you,
You are not,
Getting this.

Perception
I wish,
You could,
See through,
My eyes,
And understand,
What I see,
In you,
You've been,
Through,

So much,
And still,
Have compassion,
For other people,
Is astounding,
To behold,
For you,
To love,
Someone,
That is broken,
As me.

Adage
The symmetry,
Of you,
Is like rain,
And how,
It refreshes,
Everything,
Around it,
Your kindness,
Blossoms,
Like wildflowers,
As it spreads,
Through the lives,
Of the people you touch,
With your hands,
There's so much to you,
That there are no words,
To describe,
What it is like,
To know you,
It must be a wonder,
Being loved by you,

In the same manner,
As being kissed,
And tasting,
The lips of a beauty,
For the very first time.

Qualities
You are a dream,
A beauty,
And magic,
With haunting,
Eyes,
And voice of an angel.

Moon Dance
You're beautiful,
Don't you know,
As you climb,
The heavens at night,
Such symmetry,
It's all I can think about,
As I dance in your light,
In and out of shadows,
Just moving,
To a song,
Breaking moonbeams,
As I glide,
Along in the night,
So, here I am,
Dancing by the light,
A full moon,
Wishing you were here,

So, we could dance together,
But I know,
You are looking,
At the same moon,
And dancing too,
Wishing I was,
There with you,
Longing to feel my touch,
Just as much as I do yours.

Awe
I feel,
Like I fell,
In love,
With the moon,
So, beautiful,
To behold.
But so far,
Out of reach,
All I can do,
Is stand here,
In awe,
Of you,
Without,
Any hope,
Of holding you,
In my arms.

Tomorrow
This is something,
I've never felt,
Before,

It's fear,
I know that,
For sure,
Because,
When I stare,
Into your eyes,
I see something,
So much more,
Then your eyes,
Your mind,
Or your soul,
I see tomorrow,
Where there's we,
Not just you and I,
A family,
It shook me,
To my very core,
How do you react?
When you find,
Someone who is real,
And you feel,
Loneliness,
Awkwardness die,
Where you,
Feel yourself,
Changing,
Just from,
Her touch,
Because,
She instills,
Confidence,
Into you,
And lets you,
Be you,
While you,
Protect and love,

Her for who,
She is,
In feeling,
Someone,
And feel,
Something more,
In knowing,
That the sounds,
You hear,
Resonating,
From her,
Are the sounds,
Of your children,
Laughing,
Singing,
And calling you,
Daddy,
You see yourself,
Growing old with her,
And you're,
No longer afraid,
Of being old,
With her,
By your side.

Sparkling Moon
I love the way,
The moonlight,
Shines in your eyes,
It sparkles,
As it hangs there,
In those,
Pretty bright eyes,
Of yours,

It is so amazing,
Gazing into you,
And seeing,
The light of your soul,
Flickering,
There in your heart,
Being fed,
By the soft moonlight,
As I take your hand,
Into mine,
And dance,
Under the stars,
Looking into,
Each other's eyes,
As we move,
In the moonlight,
We see a shooting star,
And secretly,
Make a wish,
Before we kiss,
And hold each other,
Under the moonlight.

Lessoned
You can't hold,
Onto ghost,
They only slip,
Through your hands,
Because,
They are a memory,
Of things not meant to be,
So, it is best,
To leave it be,
And learn the lesson,

Don't regret things,
When it comes to people,
Missed chances,
Or lost love.

Reading
I notice things,
The subtle way,
You might say things,
The way your body,
Speaks to me,
Sometimes,
I miss the signals,
But when you,
Trip my senses,
I'm on alert,
To what,
You're thinking,
How you act,
Reading you,
Because it matters,
To understand you.

Reaction
I can't feel,
Because I am,
Numb,
From broken things,
And remain,
Un-mended,
By the pain,
I've endured,

For so long,
I hurt in silence,
Cry in the darkness,
And shiver,
Under the covers,
There's no reaction,
To all the things,
Going on,
Because,
Nothing,
Is a surprise,
Anymore,
It's expected,
Like a bad comedy,
Set on repeat.

Regrets
I once danced,
With loneliness,
We had a threesome,
Later on, in the night,
With humiliation,
Things haven't been,
The same ever since.

Schools of Rage
Two different,
Schools of thought,
Within oneself,
Sex, love, religion, and peace,
Doing right,
Being right,

And being wrong,
It's a daily battle,
Between,
Two warring factions,
It's a struggle,
Dealing with the strife,
Is sex bad, is it good,
When is it love,
Then someone,
Throws in religion,
And the machine slips gears,
Then it comes,
To a grinding halt,
Money,
Home,
Past, present and future,
All of these,
Add fuel to the fire,
Working and grinding,
It's 3 in the morning,
And the battle still rages on,
In my head,
As I fight to get to sleep.

Better
Losing you,
Was something,
I dreaded,
For the longest time,
It hurts,
But you made me,
A better man,
Than I could,
Ever be because,

Of you,
My only regret,
Was giving,
All of myself,
To you,
When you could,
Only give a small,
Portion of you,
It was such a waste,
Loosing that piece,
Of me,
That loved you,
So, much,
After all was said,
And done,
Because I never,
Felt wrong,
In loving someone,
Like you.

Beyond
You are a universe,
Complete with stars,
Suns, planets, and light,
So, beyond darkness,
Where the vastness,
Of you makes you,
Truly remarkable,
In how you create,
Life within you.

Made in the USA
Columbia, SC
06 June 2022

61309948R00083